Gun Control

Distinguishing Between Fact and Opinion

Curriculum Consultant: JoAnne Buggey, Ph.D.
College of Education, University of Minnesota

By Carol O'Sullivan

Greenhaven Press, Inc.
P.O. Box 289009
San Diego, CA 92198-0009

Titles in the opposing viewpoints juniors series:

Smoking	Death Penalty
Gun Control	Drugs and Sports
Animal Rights	Toxic Wastes
AIDS	Patriotism
Alcohol	Working Mothers
Immigration	Terrorism

Library of Congress Cataloging-in-Publication Data

Gun control : distinguishing between fact and opinion / (edited] by
   Carol O'Sullivan ; curriculum consultant, JoAnne Buggey.
         p.   cm. — (Opposing viewpoints juniors)
   Summary: Presents ten articles debating the question of whether
there should be a ban on guns.
   ISBN O-89908-638-1
   1. Gun control—United States—Juvenile literature.   [1. Gun
control.]   I. O'Sullivan, Carol, 1945– .   II. Series.
HV7436.G865 1990
363.3'3'0973—dc20   89-2226
                                                          CIP
                                                          AC

CONTENTS

An Introduction to Opposing Viewpoints

When people disagree, it is hard to figure out who is right. You may decide one person is right just because the person is your friend or a relative. But this is not a very good reason to agree or disagree with someone. It is better if you try to understand why these people disagree. On what main points do the two people disagree? Read or listen to each person's argument carefully. Separate the facts and opinions that each person presents. Finally, decide which argument best matches what you think. This process, examining an argument without emotion, is part of what critical thinking is all about.

This is not easy. Many things make it hard to understand and form opinions. People's values, ages, and experiences all influence the way they think. This is why learning to read and think critically is an invaluable skill. Opposing Viewpoints Juniors books will help

you learn and practice skills to improve your ability to read critically. By reading opposing views on an issue, you will become familiar with methods people use to attempt to convince you that their point of view is right. And you will learn to separate the authors' opinions from the facts they present.

Each Opposing Viewpoints Juniors book focuses on one critical thinking skill that will help you judge the views presented. Some of these skills are telling fact from opinion, recognizing propaganda techniques, and locating and analyzing the main idea. These skills will allow you to examine opposing viewpoints more easily. Each viewpoint in this book is paraphrased from the original to make it easier to read. The viewpoints are placed in a running debate and are always placed with the pro view first.

What Is the Difference Between Fact and Opinion?

In this Opposing Viewpoints Juniors book, you will be asked to identify and study statements of fact and statements of opinion. A fact is a statement that can be proved true. Here are some examples of factual statements: "The Statue of Liberty was dedicated in 1886 in New York," "Dinosaurs are extinct," and "George Washington was the first U.S. President." It is fairly easy to prove these facts true. For instance, a historian in the year 3000 might need to prove when the Statue of Liberty was dedicated. One way she might do this is to check in the Hall of Records in New York. She would try to find a source such as a newspaper article, the mayor's speech, or a picture of the dedication plaque to verify the date. Sometimes it is harder to check facts. In this book you will be asked to question facts in the viewpoints, and you will be given some ways in which you might go about proving them.

Statements of opinion cannot be proved. An opinion expresses how a person feels about something or what a person thinks is true. Remember the facts we mentioned? They can easily be changed into statements of opinion. For example, "Dinosaurs became extinct because a huge meteor hit the earth," "George Washington was the best president the United States ever had," and "Rebuilding the Statue of Liberty was a waste of money" are all statements of opinion. They express what one person believes to be true.

Opinions are not better than facts. They are different. Opinions are based on many things, including religious, moral, social, and family values. Opinions can also be based on facts. For instance, many scientists have made intelligent guesses about other planets based on what they know is true about earth. The only way these scientists would know their opinions were right is if they were able to visit other planets and test their guesses. Until their guesses are proved, then, they remain opinions. Some people have opinions that we do not like or with which we disagree. This does not always make their opinions wrong—or right. There is room in our world for many different opinions.

When you read differing views on any issue, it is very important to know when people are using facts and when they are using opinions in an argument. When writers use facts, their arguments are more believable and easier to prove. The more facts the author uses the more the reader can tell that the writer's opinion is based on something other than personal feelings.

Arguments that are based mostly on the author's opinions are impossible to prove factually true. This does not mean these types of arguments are not important. It means that you, as the reader, must decide whether or not you agree or disagree based on personal reasons, not factual ones.

We asked two students to give their opinions on handguns. Examine the following viewpoints. Look for facts and opinions in the arguments.

I think anyone who wants to should be allowed to own a handgun.

My dad keeps a handgun in the drawer beside his bed to protect our family. Once a man tried to break into our house while we were asleep. My dad fired a couple of shots into the air, and the man ran away. That gun probably saved our lives.

A gun is dangerous only if you don't know how to use it. Anyone can learn to use a gun. My dad taught me and my little brother how to load and fire a gun. He also taught us gun safety rules. Everyone in my family knows we should never touch a gun unless we are going to use it.

I think everyone has a right to own a gun. My dad says it's in the Constitution. No one, not even the police, should have the right to take people's guns away.

I think people should not be allowed to own handguns

People should not be allowed to keep guns in their homes. Guns are too dangerous. I've read articles in the newspaper about kids who have gotten killed by using their parents' guns. That's just stupid and sad. If the gun hadn't been in the house in the first place, the kid wouldn't have gotten killed.

Some people think that guns are good protection from burglars. I don't think that's true. When my neighbors were robbed, they weren't even home. How is a gun going to help when that happens? Plus, some burglars steal guns from people's homes and sell them to other criminals. If people are worried about burglars, they should have burglar alarms, not guns.

ANALYZING THE SAMPLE VIEWPOINTS

Steve and Sharon have different opinions about whether people should be allowed to own handguns. Both of them use examples of fact and opinion in their arguments.

Sharon:

FACTS

Once a man tried to break into our house while we were asleep.

My dad taught me and my little brother how to load and fire a gun.

OPINIONS

Anyone can learn to use a gun.

No one, not even the police, should have the right to take people's guns away.

Steve:

FACTS

I've read articles in the newspaper about kids who have gotten killed by using their parents' guns.

When my neighbors were robbed, they weren't even home.

OPINIONS

People should have burglar alarms, not guns.

Guns are too dangerous.

In this sample, Steve and Sharon both have an equal number of facts and opinions. Both Steve and Sharon think they are right about whether people should be allowed to own guns. What do you think after reading this sample? Why?

Think of two facts and two opinions that you know about guns.

As you continue to read through the viewpoints in this book, try keeping a tally like the one above to compare the authors' arguments.

CHAPTER 1

PREFACE: Should Gun Control Laws Be Passed?

Many people want tough laws controlling who is allowed to own a handgun such as a pistol or revolver. They say that if fewer people owned hand-held guns, the crime and accident rate from these weapons would drop. Supporters of tough gun laws think that, at the very least, citizens should be made to register their handguns. This means that citizens would have to notify the police when they acquire one of these weapons.

Other people believe gun control laws will not work even if they are passed. These people argue that citizens will own guns whether there is a law against it or not. The best thing to do, according to opponents of gun control, is to train citizens to use their guns properly.

In the next two viewpoints, the authors debate the gun control question.

When reading these two viewpoints, use your critical thinking skills to find the facts and opinions each author presents. Which case is more strongly based on fact? Which on opinion?

Editor's Note: This viewpoint is paraphrased from an article by Edward F. Dolan Jr., an author. In this reading, he gives three arguments to prove gun control is necessary. Pay close attention to the facts the author uses.

Many people are against gun control laws. They argue that gun control laws will not work because criminals do not obey the law anyway. These people believe that gun control will not stop a criminal from getting a gun. While this may be true, most handgun murders are not committed by criminals. They are committed by ordinary people in the heat of an argument.

A 1980 F.B.I. report found that 51 percent of the murders in the United States were committed by family members or acquaintances during an argument. There is one way to stop these senseless "crimes of passion," and that is to make laws forbidding the use of a handgun. Then the gun will not be there when someone flies into a rage.

What does the author believe would prevent crimes of passion? Is this a fact or an opinion?

These same facts are also true about suicide. People who have decided to commit suicide would have more time to change their minds if they did not have handguns. Strict gun control laws would also prevent accidents that happen in the home when a gun is present.

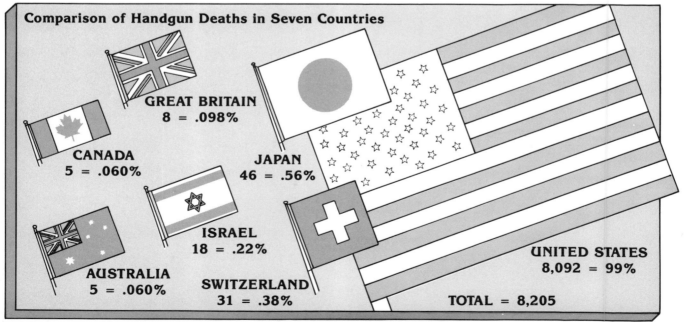

Comparison of Handgun Deaths in Seven Countries

GREAT BRITAIN
8 = .098%

CANADA
5 = .060%

JAPAN
46 = .56%

ISRAEL
18 = .22%

AUSTRALIA
5 = .060%

SWITZERLAND
31 = .38%

UNITED STATES
8,092 = 99%

TOTAL = 8,205

SOURCE: Handgun Control 1985

Cities with strict gun control laws have lower crime rates. Both Philadelphia, Pennsylvania, and Toledo, Ohio, have gun control laws.

In Philadelphia, every citizen who applies for a gun permit must register with the police department. Before issuing a permit, the police check to see if the person has committed any crimes. In one year, the police department found twenty-seven people who had been convicted of violent crimes; sixty-nine with past records for carrying concealed weapons; and close to two hundred with robbery, theft, rape, and drug addiction records.

CREDIT: Reprinted by permission of UFS, Inc.

Toledo has a similar law. After just two years, the handgun murder rate dropped by 22 percent. This proves gun control laws lower the crime rate.

Statistics from foreign countries also prove gun control works well.

In Great Britain, before people are allowed to buy a gun, they must have certificates that prove they can use a handgun properly. The British believe their strong gun control laws and their punishments for people who do not obey these laws have kept the murder rate low.

Japan completely outlawed the possession of handguns by its citizens. The murder rate there is even lower than in Great Britain. In 1972, Japan, a country of 107 million people, had only twenty-eight handgun murders. In contrast, 10,000 people in the United States died in handgun murders.

In France, anyone who plans to buy a gun must first undergo a thorough police investigation. In the Netherlands, people are required to get a permit to own a gun. Five European countries totally ban handguns. They are Albania, Cyprus, Greece, Ireland, and the Soviet Union. Gun control laws have all worked to reduce crime in these countries. They can do the same for us.

What facts does the author use to prove gun control can lower the crime rate?

Does the Japan statistic prove that outlawing handguns will lower the murder rate?

Do gun control laws work?

Mr. Dolan presents three arguments in favor of gun control. What are these three arguments? What facts does he use to support these arguments? Do you agree with Mr. Dolan that gun control works? Why or why not?

Editor's Note: This viewpoint is paraphrased from an article by Don Feder, editor of *On Principle,* a newsletter. In this article, Mr. Feder explains why he is against gun control laws.

SOURCE: Bob Dix, *Manchester Union Leader.*
Reprinted with permission.

300,000 seems like a lot of people. Actually, it is less than one percent of the U.S. population. What is the author trying to prove by using this statistic? Does the statistic make his point?

Many people who want strong gun control laws say that a handgun is not a good weapon for defense against criminals. These people argue that studies have shown that people who own guns are more likely to kill someone they know rather than an attacker.

It may be true that some people have misused their handguns. But studies also show that, with training, anyone can learn to use a handgun for self-defense.

One study done by a research company says that each year 300,000 Americans use handguns to defend themselves. In fact, every national police organization says people can learn to use handguns for self-defense. These groups include the International Association of Chiefs of Police, the National Sheriffs Association, and the National Police Officers Association of America.

People who favor gun control laws also argue that these laws would prevent a person from shooting a friend or acquaintance in the heat of an argument. These people think that if the law forbids citizens to own guns they will not own them. Then, when these citizens get into an argument with an acquaintance, there will not be a gun in the house. Nobody will get shot.

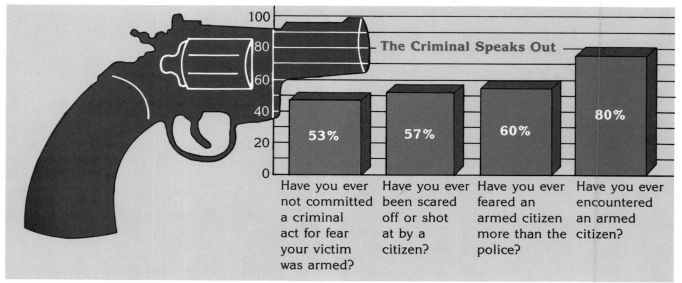

SOURCE: James Wright and Peter Rossi 1985

But this is a faulty argument. Most people who want to own a gun will own one whether there is a law against it or not. New York's failure to enforce its gun control law proves this. This law, called the Sullivan law, was passed in 1911. It requires that all handguns be registered. In spite of this law, there are one to two million unregistered handguns in New York.

Supporters of gun control point out countries and cities where it has worked to lower the crime rate. But they ignore the places where crime rates have increased since gun control laws went into effect. For example, Boston, Massachusetts, once had the fifth highest crime rate in the U.S. In 1976, Massachusetts passed a gun control law. This law says a person must go to jail for a year for carrying an unlicensed hand gun. Five years later, in 1981, Boston had the highest crime rate in the U.S. It is obvious that handgun laws do not work in Boston. Why would they work anywhere else?

Gun control supporters are always arguing that Great Britain, a country with strict gun control laws, has a low crime rate. But these people do not mention that the British had an even lower crime rate before they had gun control laws.

Also, America's rate of homicide (the killing of one person by another, whether accidentally or on purpose) increased 30 percent from 1960 to 1975. Great Britain's rose 50 percent. So, Great Britain's crime rate increased even more than America's, even though Great Britain has stricter gun control laws than America has.

It would be nice to think that passing strict gun control laws would solve the crime problem in the United States. But the facts show that gun control will not work. Rather than trying to take people's guns away from them, we should be trying to teach them how to use their guns.

Why does the author think people will own guns whether the law forbids it or not? Is his reason based on fact or opinion?

Do you think that New York's inability to enforce its gun control law proves that most people who want to own a handgun will own one? Why or why not?

What facts does the author think are ignored by people who support gun control? Do you think these facts are important?

What conclusion does the author make about gun control laws? Is this conclusion a fact or an opinion? Why?

Would gun control laws lower the crime rate?

Mr. Feder presents three arguments against gun control laws. What are these three arguments? What facts does he use to support these arguments? Do you agree with Mr. Feder that gun control laws do not lower the crime rate? Why or why not?

Tallying the Facts and Opinions

After reading the two viewpoints on gun control, make a chart similar to the one made for Steve and Sharon on page 8. List the facts and opinions each author gives to make his case. A chart is started for you below:

Dolan:

FACTS

Seventy percent of the people killed by handguns are killed by people they know.

OPINIONS

It is nonsense to believe a gun can protect you against crime.

Feder:

FACTS

Each year 300,000 Americans use handguns to defend themselves.

OPINIONS

This is a faulty argument.

Which article used more factual statements? Which did you think was the most convincing? Why?

2

PREFACE: Does the Constitution Guarantee the Right to Own Guns?

The Second Amendment to the Constitution of the United States was ratified on December 15, 1791. It says:

> "A well-regulated militia, being necessary to the security of a free State, the right of the people to keep and bear arms, shall not be infringed."

Some people think these words mean that only people in the United States military services can own guns. Other people say the words mean that all people of the United States can own guns.

In the next two viewpoints, the authors debate which interpretation of the Second Amendment is correct.

When reading these viewpoints, pay attention to the authors' facts and opinions on these issues.

Editor's Note: This viewpoint is paraphrased from an article by Charley Reese, a journalist. In this article, Mr. Reese explains why he thinks the Constitution allows private citizens to own guns.

The Second Amendment to the Constitution of the United States says people have the right to keep and bear arms. This means citizens can own guns.

Some people think this amendment allows only members of the military the right to own guns. These people are idiots. I will prove that the Second Amendment says any citizen can own a gun.

In 1776, citizens of the United States declared their independence from Great Britain. At this time, leaders of the United States wrote the Declaration of Independence. This document lists rights that apply to all Americans. This includes today's Americans.

Bob Dix, *Manchester Union Leader.* Reprinted with permission.

One of these rights is that Americans are allowed to form a government. Another right Americans have is the right to get rid of the government when it is not doing its job. This means Americans can even use weapons to overthrow the government if they have to. After all, it would not make sense to say people have the right to overthrow the government if they do not have the weapons to do it.

About fifteen years after American leaders wrote the Declaration of Independence, they wrote the Second Amendment to the Constitution. They based their ideas for this amendment on the ideas in the Declaration of Independence. They included in the amendment the right of the people to get rid of the government—by force if necessary. Therefore, they intended for people to own guns, even handguns, if they want to.

These facts prove that the Second Amendment allows all citizens to own guns. It is foolish to think that this right is just for members of the military.

What facts does the author use in this paragraph? How might you go about proving these facts?

Is this statement a fact or an opinion? Why?

Do you agree that the facts prove this?

Guns and the second amendment

List two facts Mr. Reese uses to support his argument that the Second Amendment allows private citizens to own handguns. List two opinions.

What rights does Mr. Reese say the Declaration of Independence gives to all Americans? Do you think these rights include the right to own a handgun? Why or why not?

The Constitution does not guarantee the right to own guns

Some people believe that the Second Amendment to the United States Constitution grants all people living in America today the right to own a gun. This is not true. We can go back into history and see why.

The men who wrote the Second Amendment did intend for citizens living during their time to own guns, including handguns. They allowed citizens to own guns to defend the country in case of enemy attack. This was because the government could not afford to pay a full-time army.

Peanuts

CREDIT: Reprinted by permission of UFS, Inc.

But today, America has a military budget of nearly $300 billion. This includes money to pay a full-time army. The country does not need a military made up of citizens to defend it. Therefore, today's citizens do not need guns.

Common sense tells us that the Second Amendment does not give all Americans living today the right to own a gun. It is time we learned the real meaning of this amendment.

What facts do the authors give in this paragraph?

What is the authors' conclusion? Is it fact or opinion? Why?

Dana Summers. Reprinted by permission.

HANDS ACROSS AMERICA

Do citizens need guns?

List two facts the authors use to support the argument that the Second Amendment does not allow private citizens to own guns. List two opinions.

According to the authors, why did the men who wrote the Second Amendment allow all citizens to own guns? Why do the authors think this right does not apply today? Do you agree or disagree?

Analyzing Gun Advertising

PORTRAIT OF A FELLOW AMERICAN EXERCISING HIS "CONSTITUTIONAL RIGHTS"

NATIONAL COALITION TO BAN HANDGUNS
100 Maryland Avenue N E
Washington D C 20002

National Coalition to Ban Handguns

Each one of us sees and hears dozens of advertising messages every day. Some of these ads tell us to use a product because it will do something for us, like make us safe. Some ads tell us we should outlaw certain products because they are too dangerous. One product often advertised in these ways is the handgun. This activity will help you analyze such messages.

Look at ad number one. What is its message? Would this ad change your mind if you owned a handgun? Why or why not? How does this ad affect you personally? Do you think the ad is effective? Do you think the ad would be as effective if the gun were not pointed at you? Why or why not?

Now, look at ad number two. What is its message? How does it contrast with the message in ad number one? Why is the man wearing a stocking over his face? Do you think the ad is effective? Would this ad change your mind if you were opposed to owning a handgun? Why or why not?

After looking at both ads, decide which message you would pay more attention to. Why?

At times like this, don't you wish you owned a handgun?

3

PREFACE: **Are Handguns Too Dangerous to Be Kept in Homes?**

Most people agree that the crime rate in the United States is too high. But they disagree over whether the benefits of keeping a handgun in the home for self-defense outweigh the problems caused by owning such a weapon.

Accidental shootings are one of the problems that sometimes result when a handgun is kept in the home for self-defense. Crimes of passion (shootings committed in the heat of an argument) are another. A third problem is suicide. People who are against keeping a handgun in the home say there is one way to stop these senseless shootings—keep handguns out of the home.

People who support handgun ownership believe there are many advantages to keeping handguns in the home. In some cases, homeowners have scared away criminals with their handguns. In other cases, the homeowner simply feels safer with a handgun in the house. Handgun supporters believe it is possible to keep a gun in the house for safety without having it cause problems.

The next two viewpoints discuss these issues. When reading these two viewpoints, pay attention to the authors' facts and opinions.

Handguns can be kept in most homes

Editor's Note: This viewpoint is paraphrased from an article by James D. Wright, professor of sociology at the University of Massachusetts. In it, he argues that handguns can safely be kept in the home.

Many people oppose keeping a handgun in the home to prevent crime. They argue that handguns are useless for protection against crime.

These people cite a study done by George Newton and Franklin Zimring. This study reports that handguns prevent criminals from breaking into houses only two out of one thousand times. But the study ignores an important fact. If a criminal thinks a homeowner owns and can use a handgun, he probably will not break in. No crime will be committed. Therefore, the gun foiled the crime just by being in the house.

People who oppose handgun ownership also argue that guns are too dangerous to keep in the house. They say people use handguns to shoot family members and acquaintances during arguments.

But it is possible that many of these shootings, called "crimes of passion," are not really accidental. They may be premeditated. The attacker may have planned to shoot the victim all along. There are cases where people have started fights just to have an excuse to shoot a relative or acquaintance.

Why does the author criticize this study? Is his criticism a fact or an opinion? Why?

Law Enforcement Officers Speak Out

"I think that gun control legislation"...

has no effect on crime
79.1%

reduces crime somewhat
10.0%

substantially reduces crime
1.2%

increases crime
4.4%

No opinion
5.3%

SOURCE: National-International Market & Opinion Research

Some people also argue that accidental shootings happen when guns are kept in the house. Most of these accidents are caused by children who find the gun. Maybe people with youngsters should not own guns. But that does not mean guns can not be safely kept in houses where there are no young children.

There is a final reason some people oppose keeping a handgun in the house. They say the benefits of keeping a gun in the house are psychological. They argue that the feelings of being safer is only in people's minds and that, actually, people are not safer at all.

But feeling safer is a good reason to keep a handgun in the house. If people feel safer because they own a gun, they will lead happier lives.

Handguns may be dangerous in some circumstances. They may be useless in others. But there are many circumstances in which a handgun can be a valuable weapon for self-defense. These situations make it all right for most people to keep a handgun in the house.

Are these statements fact or opinion? How might you go about proving those statements that are facts?

What point is the author making about the benefits of owning a gun? Do you agree or disagree?

What is the author's conclusion? Is it fact or opinion?

Fatal Home Accidents

Drowning 700

Firearms 800

Suffocation 2,500

All others 2,600

Poisoning 3,800

Fire 4,000

Falls 6,100

20,500 TOTAL FATAL HOME ACCIDENTS

SOURCE: National Safety Council

Handguns in the home

List three facts and three opinions Mr. Wright gives to support his view that handguns can be valuable for self-defense.

The author gives four reasons some people are against keeping a handgun in the house. What are these four reasons? What facts does the author use to argue against each of these reasons?

Handguns should not be kept in the home

Editor's Note: This viewpoint is paraphrased from an article by Jervis Anderson, a writer for *The New Yorker* magazine. In it, he argues that handguns are too dangerous to keep in the home.

What does the author say about the crime rate in the U.S.? Is this a fact or an opinion? What facts does he use to support this statement?

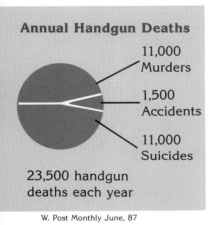

Annual Handgun Deaths

11,000 Murders

1,500 Accidents

11,000 Suicides

23,500 handgun deaths each year

W. Post Monthly June, 87

Millions of people in the United States own handguns for self-defense. This is understandable. The murder rate in this country is exorbitant. Between 1963 and 1973, 84,644 U.S. citizens were killed by guns. Most were killed with handguns. In 1981 there was one violent crime committed in America every twenty-four seconds. Many of these were handgun murders.

People fear crime. And they are tired of being victims. As one homeowner said, "I've worked too hard to get what I've got to let anybody take it away from me."

It is true that we need to do something to protect ourselves against crime. But a handgun is too dangerous a weapon to keep around the house. Too often, the gun is used to shoot a family member or acquaintance rather than to shoot a criminal.

Sometimes the shooting is accidental. For example, in New York a four-year-old girl shot and wounded her two-year-old brother. She thought the gun was a toy.

Also in New York, an actress shot herself in the stomach. She was trying to unload a handgun.

Reprinted with permission

While some of the shootings are accidental, some are intentional. According to the F.B.I., 55 percent of the murders committed in 1981 were by relatives or persons who knew the victims.

For example, in Georgia a thirteen-year-old boy was depressed because his parents were getting a divorce. He held a gun to his head and threatened to shoot. His mother begged him to shoot her instead. He did.

Accidental shootings and shooting of acquaintances are enough reason to keep handguns out of the home. But there is another reason. People use them to commit suicide.

The New England Journal of Medicine reported that 83 percent of the guns used in suicides in 1983 were handguns. This study also said, "The rise in the suicide rate might be controlled" if people did not own handguns.

There is a final danger of owning handguns for self-defense. This peril is to our whole society. Guns kept in the home are sometimes stolen by criminals during break-ins. Then they are used by the criminals to commit more crimes. Therefore, the more guns there are in houses, the more guns are likely to end up in the hands of criminals.

Many people believe guns should be removed from our society. The Assistant District Attorney of Los Angeles agrees that we must eliminate handguns. He says, "There are too many guns in our community, and . . . too many people are willing to use them."

It is obvious that too many people get injured or killed by the guns meant to protect them. Guns bought for self-defense do more harm to innocent people than they do to criminals. This is too high a price to pay for keeping a gun in the house.

Are these examples of accidental and intentional shootings facts or opinions? Why?

What facts does the author use in this paragraph? What is his point?

What point is the author making in this conclusion? Is this a fact or an opinion? Do you agree or disagree?

Are handguns dangerous?

List three facts and three opinions that help support Mr. Anderson's view that the dangers of owning a handgun for self-defense outweigh the benefits.

Mr. Anderson agrees that we need to protect ourselves against crime. But he disagrees that using a handgun is the best way to protect ourselves. Can you think of any ways we could protect ourselves from criminals without using weapons?

Distinguishing Between Fact and Opinion

The following sentences are based on information contained in the readings. Write "F" beside those sentences that are facts and "O" beside those sentences that are opinions.

EXAMPLE: Most handgun murders are committed by ordinary people in the heat of an argument.   **F**

1. It would be nice to think that passing strict gun control laws would solve the crime problem in the United States.   _____

2. America's homicide rate increased 30 percent from 1960 to 1975.   _____

3. A 1980 F.B.I. report found that 51 percent of the murders in the United States were committed by family members or acquaintances during an argument.   _____

4. Rather than trying to take people's guns away from them, we should be trying to teach them how to use their guns.   _____

5. Gun registration will not keep handguns away from criminals.   _____

6. The Assistant District Attorney of Los Angeles agrees we must eliminate handguns.   _____

CHAPTER

PREFACE: Are Handguns the Best Weapons for Self-Defense?

Fifty million handguns are circulating in our society today. Some of these are owned by criminals, but most are owned by law-abiding, peace-loving citizens. In fact, recent polls show that more than half the households in the United States have at least one gun.

With so many guns in our society, it is likely that the lives of nearly every citizen of the United States will somehow be touched by a gun. He or she may own a gun or be the victim of an accident or crime committed with a gun. Perhaps he or she will know someone who becomes a gun victim.

The authors of the following viewpoints have in some way experienced violence caused by a handgun. One author had a friend who was shot and killed by a burglar; the other was forced to shoot a mugger.

In these viewpoints, each author shares his feelings of sadness and outrage at the violence in our society. And each believes we need to defend ourselves from criminals. But each author has a different idea about what kind of weapon is most effective for use against criminals.

When reading these viewpoints, pay close attention to each author's conclusion about why handguns do or do not make good weapons for self-defense. Also, determine which author uses more facts from sources other than his own experiences.

A handgun is a good weapon for self-defense

Editor's Note: This viewpoint is paraphrased from an article by Chip Elliot, a novelist. In it he tells a personal story that convinced him that handguns are needed for self-defense.

What is the author's point of view about whether or not we live in a safe society? Is this fact or opinion?

GO AHEAD. MAKE MY DAY!

THE EQUALIZER

CREDIT: Don Eckelkamp, The New American. Reprinted with permission.

We are living in a world where self-defense is necessary. I used to have trouble accepting this. But now I carry a 9mm Smith and Wesson automatic. Several things happened to me to cause me to buy a handgun.

It began one morning. I was sitting on the front porch of my house in Venice, California. I watched a gang of teenagers pour gasoline all over a parked car and set it on fire. It was broad daylight.

A few days later a woman went to the door of a neighbor's house and asked if she could use the phone. My neighbor let her in. Some men came in right behind her and stabbed my neighbor to death.

After hearing these stories, my wife and I decided to buy a small handgun—a .38-caliber snub-nosed revolver. Nothing had happened to us personally, but we wanted to be on the safe side. We put the gun under the corner of our mattress and forgot about it.

Then one night we came home from the movies and found that our house had been burglarized. The stereo, television, paintings, camera, and typewriters were gone. The burglars had let the parakeet out of its cage, and the cat ate it. They got the gun, too. Our revolver had now entered the underworld.

So we bought another gun. This time we bought a big .38 Special Smith and Wesson.

Up to this point, I had never been threatened physically. So I don't know why one night I decided to take the gun with me just to go out for a beer. But I did.

Coming back home, I was stopped by five teenagers. I don't have a lot of money. I don't look like I have a lot of money. So I thought, "What do you guys want with me?"

Their leader pulled a kitchen knife out of his leather jacket. He smiled at me and said, "Just the wallet, man. Won't be no trouble."

I looked at this guy and his friends for a minute. Then I pulled the handgun, leveled it at them, and said very clearly, "You must be dreaming."

The guy smiled at me and said, "sheeeeit." He moved toward me with his knife. I thought, "This guy is willing to kill me for thirty-five dollars."

I aimed the handgun at the outer edge of his left thigh and shot him.

"Damn," he yelled. Then he yelled at this buddies, "Ain't you gonna do nothing?" They did nothing.

I backed off and walked home. "Shouldn't I call a doctor?" I asked myself. And then I thought, "Would he have called a doctor for me?" And I kept right on walking.

I'm not proud of this. I couldn't even tell my wife about it until a year later. But I did it. And I would do it again if I had to.

So this is what caused me to go from doubting that we need handguns for self-defense to being convinced that handguns are necessary. And they will be necessary until our fellow citizens get it out of their heads that they can do as they please. Because, the way I see it, if they have the right to mug us, we have the right to shoot them.

So now we have another problem. How can we keep all these handguns from falling into the hands of criminals? I'm not sure we can. Some people think we can control who owns handguns by making gun owners register them. I would like to believe that this would keep handguns away from criminals. But it won't. Most criminals get their guns by stealing them. This makes registration useless.

Unfortunately, we live in a society where many people think they can do whatever they damn please. They have no sense of morality. These people think no one will stop them. They're right. No one will—not the police, not the courts, not the jails. No one will stop them except the growing number of us who have decided we will never be victims of crime again.

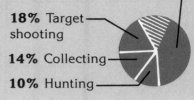

Reasons Citizens Give for Owning Handguns

58% Protection (14% have **used** for self-defense)

18% Target shooting

14% Collecting

10% Hunting

SOURCE: Decision Making Information 1978

What led the author to believe that guns are necessary? Are these facts or opinions?

The author says most criminals get their guns by what method? Is this fact or opinion? How might you go about proving this statement?

Is the author's conclusion fact or opinion? Why? Do you agree or disagree?

Handguns and self-defense

To convince us that people need handguns for self-defense, Mr. Elliot tells a story about events that happened in his own life. He uses very few facts from other sources. Do you think this use of "first person point of view," or telling about his personal experience, makes his argument strong or weak? Why?

Do you think Mr. Elliot should have shot the teenager? Why or why not?

Editor's Note: This viewpoint is paraphrased from an article by Adam Smith, a journalist. In it, he tells why he thinks shotguns are better weapons than handguns for self-defense.

What point does the author make about how Americans feel about violence in their society? Is this a fact or an opinion? What evidence does he use to prove his point? Is this evidence fact or opinion?

H. Rap Brown, the civil rights activist, once said, "Violence is as American as apple pie." I guess he is right. Four of our presidents died violently. We make heroes of thieves and murderers like Butch Cassidy and the Sundance Kid. But we do not remember the names of the trainmen and bank clerks they killed.

I have seen a lot of crime in my own lifetime. A friend of mine was a victim of violent crime. His name was Dr. Michael Halberstam. He was a heart specialist in Washington, D.C. A burglar broke into Halberstam's home and shot him. Halberstam managed to get into his car and run down the burglar. But he died soon after. A few days later, John Lennon, a member of the Beatles rock group, was gunned down in New York City.

These deaths made me sad and angry. But I do not believe that using handguns for self-defense will stop these violent murders. The facts prove this. There are fifty million handguns in this country. But the murder rate has not decreased. Another two million handguns will be sold this year. I will bet the murder rate still does not go down.

What facts does the author use in this paragraph? What is his point?

I am not against owning any gun for self-defense. I am just against owning a handgun. Handguns are sometimes stolen from the home and used to commit other crimes. In fact, half of all guns used in crimes are stolen. Seventy percent of them are handguns.

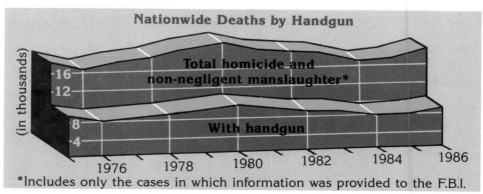

Nationwide Deaths by Handgun

*Includes only the cases in which information was provided to the F.B.I.

SOURCE: Federal Bureau of Investigation

Shotguns are much better weapons to use for self-defense. You have to be an excellent shot to shoot someone with a handgun. But almost anyone can shoot a person with a shotgun. Also, shotguns are safer to keep in the house. Criminals hardly ever steal shotguns and use them to commit other crimes.

Maybe someday people will get together and finally agree that handguns are the best weapons for self-defense. If this happens, I think people should have to register their handguns. Registration may not stop criminals from owning guns. But we have to do something to control who owns handguns. Registration is a good beginning. We make drivers get licenses and register their cars. That does not stop automobile deaths. But I am convinced that the highways would be even more dangerous if they were filled with unlicensed drivers and unregistered cars.

Crime is certainly a problem in this country. But there is an even bigger problem. We have gotten so used to crime and violence that we have begun to accept it. We become angry over senseless deaths, like that of John Lennon, but we soon forget them. Then things go right on as they did before.

We must do more than just force people to register their handguns. We must find ways to make people understand that they cannot just do whatever they please. We have to convince them that they do not have the right to harm others or steal.

Why does the author think shotguns make better weapons than handguns? Are his reasons facts or opinions?

What does the author think is an even bigger problem than crime in the United States? Is this fact or opinion?

Do you think it is possible to make people change the way they behave? How might you go about doing this?

Violence in America

Can you list three facts the author gives to support his view that handguns are not good weapons for self-defense? Can you list three opinions?

Mr. Smith thinks Americans accept violence as part of their society. Do you agree or disagree? Can you think of any organizations, laws, situations, or other evidence that suggest Americans are opposed to violence?

Understanding Editorial Cartoons

Throughout this book you have seen cartoons that illustrate the ideas in the viewpoints. Editorial cartoons are an effective and usually humorous way of presenting an opinion on an issue. While many cartoons are easy to understand, others, like the one below, may require more thought. The cartoon below deals with the danger of children getting hold of guns kept in the home. It is similar to the cartoons that appear in your daily newspaper.

Look at the cartoon. Do you think the cartoonist believes guns should be kept in homes where there are children? Why or why not? Do you agree with the cartoonist? Why or why not?

Don Wright, *Miami News*. Reprinted with permission.